The Third Reich Bravery and Merit Decoration for Eastern Peoples

Rolf Michaelis

Schiffer Publishing Ltd

4880 Lower Valley Road • Atglen, PA 19310

Library of Congress Control Number: 2014946926

Designed by Robert Biondi and Rolf Michaelis
Type set in Georgia/Gill Sans Std

ISBN: 978-0-7643-4803-7
Printed in China

Published by Schiffer Publishing, Ltd.
4880 Lower Valley Road
Atglen, PA 19310
Phone: (610) 593-1777; Fax: (610) 593-2002
E-mail: Info@schifferbooks.com

Translated from the German by David Johnston.

This book was originally published under the title,
Die Tapferkeits- und Verdienstauszeichnung für Angehörige der Ostvölker,
@ 1997 by Michaelis-Verlag, Berlin, Germany.

Contents

Foreword....4

The Eastern European Volunteers....5

The Decoration for Bravery and Merit for Eastern Peoples....12

Bibliography....19

Foreword

Between the summer of 1941 and the end of the war, hundreds of thousands of Soviet volunteers served in the German military, the *Waffen-SS* and police, with and without weapons, as "members of the Eastern peoples."

As Hitler did not soften his policies toward the Eastern volunteers until 1942-43, by which time the tide of the war had turned against Germany, it was no simple matter to honor their contributions. Awarding of the Iron Cross or War Merit Cross was initially forbidden and was later only undertaken in exceptional circumstances.

To recognize the service of the steadily growing number of eastern volunteers, however, about a year after the start of the war in Russia, Hitler approved the introduction of a bravery and merit decoration for members of the eastern peoples.

Even though the decoration isolated the foreigners because, in principle, it was issued only to them and not to Germans, it was at least a step toward recognizing their accomplishments.

Those eastern units that saw combat were, as a rule, more poorly equipped than German units. Nevertheless, some units fought more desperately than German formations, because they knew that they could expect no pardon from the Red Army.

Regardless of whether they were opportunists or idealists, when the German Reich surrendered, almost all of the eastern volunteers fell into Stalin's hands and faced the most severe reprisals: years of forced labor and death.

Rolf Michaelis
Erlangen, August 1997

The Eastern European Volunteers

"Operation Barbarossa," the German invasion of the Soviet Union, began on 21 June 1941. It was a war between ideologies which, though completely antithecal, shared common objectives. For Hitler and leading Nazis it was also a war to destroy Jewish-Bolshevik society and oppress the Slavs. Conscious of the fact that many residents of the Soviet state would volunteer to fight communism, on 16 July 1942 Hitler declared:

> *"The iron-clad rule must be and remain: no one but Germans must ever be permitted to bear arms! This is especially important; even if it initially appears easier to enlist the military assistance of some foreign subject people, it is wrong! One day they will absolutely and inevitably spurn us. Only the German may carry arms, not the Slav, not the Czech, not the Cossack nor the Ukrainian."*

Despite this official declaration, the German command quietly permitted Latvian and Estonian volunteer units and foreign auxiliaries to serve in various German units. Then, in autumn 1941, so-called eastern legions were from members of non-Slavic minorities in the south of the USSR, most of which had suffered under communism. Then, as the military situation worsened, in 1942 Hitler authorized so-called eastern units made up of Slavic volunteers. The reason for Hitler's change of heart can be discerned in a letter from the OKH on 18 August 1942:

> *"The size of the eastern area and the imperative to conserve German lives have forced us to enlist the forces of the conquered lands in the east, as well as prisoners of war, to serve in the Wehrmacht and the war economy."*

Consequently, units were raised from inhabitants not evacuated by Stalin and discharged prisoners of war. Most members of both groups who could not be used in a combat role were employed in the armaments industry, where they endured inhumane treatment.

Whether an eastern people was used in an armed role was basically determined by its origins:

> Persons from the Caucasus (Turkmen, Uzbeks, Kazaks, Kyrgyzes, Karakalpaks, Tajiks, Azerbaizhanis, Armenians, Georgians, Cherkessens, Adiges, Karbardins, Abkhazians, Karachayans, Balkarians, North-Ossetians, Ingushians, Chechens, Dagestanians, Volga Tatars and Bashkirians) and Cossacks fought at the front and against partisans in Eastern Legions with German core personnel.
>
> Estonians, Latvians, Lithuanians, White Ruthenes, Russians and Ukrainians served in the war against partisans in domestic security units (Eastern Units).

Russian and Ukrainian police units were also attached to the *Ordnungspolizei* (auxiliary police) and carried out police duties.

Members of the eastern peoples were also employed as unarmed auxiliaries in varying numbers in German divisions, in some cases accounting for 10% of the unit's strength.

Men from the eastern territories volunteered for three main reasons: on one hand, various peoples had been disadvantaged in the USSR and oppressed by Moscow. For this reason many men wanted to help bring about Stalin's downfall – possibly in the hope of an independent state after a German victory. On thc other hand, the Germans behaved so badly in the occupied areas that many volunteered to avoid deportation. Among Soviet prisoners of war, however, the experience of starvation in 1941-42 and the resulting mass deaths may have been the main motive. Hundreds of thousands of Soviet POWs died of exhaustion and sickness at that time.

The volunteers therefore had a variety of motivations, and this led to major differences in operational capabilities. The following report by *the SS-Sonderbataillon Dirlewanger* to *SS-Obergruppenführer* von dem Bach, who was responsible for the anti-partisan war, describes such conditions:

> *"In the appendix, the unit has included a report by the SD hunting detachment attached to the SS-Sonderbataillon concerning the approximately 280 black police in and around Lohoysk. Concerning the report, it should be explained that:*
>
> *During the SS-Sonderbataillon's absence during "Operation Draufgänger II," another 120 police were sent to Lohoysk in addition to the approximately 280 already there. If conditions there were almost unbearable before, after the arrival of these 120 new men they were almost impossible to control militarily. Almost hourly, farmers from the surrounding villages came to report plundering by these completely undisciplined fellows. The SD team assigned to the SS-Sonderbataillon had to send three men back to Lohoysk to investigate at least some of these complaints. The SS-Sonderbataillon had to reinforce its remaining guards in Lohoysk in order to reduce thefts in the unit's quarters and at the same time ensure that the undisciplined horde did not make common cause with the bandits [partisans].*

During "Operation Lenz-Nord," the SS-Sonderbataillon and the SD thoroughly investigated the recruiting methods described in the SD's report. The following was properly established:

When the SS-Sonderbataillon was in the assigned bandit villages, several dozen black police from Lohoysk appeared, moved into the neighboring bandit villages and declared to the residents there that the SS was near, and that in keeping with standard practice it would burn down the villages and shoot the residents. If the men of the village wanted to save their lives, they could join the black police that day.

Afterwards it was impossible to determine how often this happened, because the population completely abandoned these villages after the arrival of the black auxiliary police. All were bandit villages in which bandits or suspected bandits known to the SD were supposed to be rounded up and shot... These strange recruiting methods made it impossible for the SD to carry out its mission, however, because the male band members or suspected bandits had either already become black policemen or had hidden in the forests.

When, during "Operation Draufgänger II," the SS-Sonderbataillon tried to consult with the German officers in charge of these 120 men, this proved impossible. The military police Oberleutnant's deputy had gone to Minsk that day (it was probably the 8th of May), his deputy had also gone to Minsk on leave, and the third gendarme left in the village declared that he was only responsible for seven of these fellows.

The 280 black police in the village also represent a military threat that cannot be underestimated, because the way they were recruited leads one to suspect that they are still cooperating with the bandits, and because their numbers are out of all proportion to the German military police assigned to supervise them. There are five German gendarmes in Lohoysk, two of them are presently on leave, one is on detached duty, one prepares the food, the last sits in the office. The auxiliary police are therefore always on their own and completely unsupervised.

The SS-Sonderbataillon has succeeded in turning the battalion's two Russian companies into disciplined, eager units. The battalion has so far had just one deserter, but 52 dead and wounded Russians. This is because in the Russian companies, for every eight Russians there is one German, who lives, sleeps, eats and goes into the field with the Russians. However, a unit where there are 280 blacks with almost no Germans is unacceptable. To avoid unpleasant incidents, is requested that an order be issued to the effect that no more than 50 blacks remain in Lohoysk, and that the rest be immediately stripped of their uniforms, disarmed and sent to Germany to work.

In conclusion, it must be mentioned that the poor example of the black auxiliary police is having a demoralizing effect on the two Russian companies, because these so-called black guards are often found asleep in broad daylight and because these guards frequently put down their rifles to spend time with a girl near their guard area."

A former member of the 828th Volga Tatar Battalion remembered:

"After a very impressive conversation with Major Meyer-Mader, I volunteered to serve in the Eastern Legions. As an Oberzahlmeister, I was attached to the 929th Volga Tatar Battalion from the time of its formation in autumn 1942 until I was sent away to retrain as a company grade officer in my old branch, the anti-tank guns, in spring 1944.

The German core personnel (approx. 10% of the unit's strength) were mostly soldiers with experience at the front, but they were not sufficiently prepared to deal with very different kinds of men who had been members of the Russia and who could never be made into Prussian grenadiers, and they had also not been selected for personal suitability. Some had also been affected by National-Socialist "subhuman" propaganda. Many Germans therefore often referred to the legionnaires as "Kuschnoken" [a derogatory term for Slavic people].

The main reason why the eastern legions failed to live up to the expectations of their advocates and promoters was because the legionnaires had only so much willingness. The weapons and equipment they were issued was not up to the latest German standards and was largely captured material. The battalion headquarters staff (commanding officer, adjutant, aide-de-camp, doctor, paymaster and interpreter – a Sonderführer (Z) with the rank of a Leutnant) was German. In the 828th Volga Tatar Infantry Battalion, only the 1st and 4th (Machine-Gun) Companies had German commanders. The remaining companies were led by Tatars who had held similar positions in the Red Army. In each case they were assisted by a German company advisor. Most of the latter were Oberfeldwebel who had been awarded the Iron Cross, First Class.

At that time our battalion was used to guard the Drohobycz oil region (Galicia) and fight partisans. The Volga Tatar legionnaires employed the same ruthlessness against the partisans that the latter displayed in the struggle against the Germans and their allies. Their reliability declined as the war went on and the scales increasingly shifted in favor of the Soviets. In one case, this led to the commander of the

Headquarters Company dissolving the strongpoint manned by his legionnaires. The German NCOs there were disarmed, stripped and tied up, before the legionnaires disappeared in the direction of the Red Army.

As far as the legionnaires' level of training is concerned, it can be said that in general it was at the lower limit of average. Of course there was political instruction by the eastern propagandists and also by the mullahs (prayer leaders) in each company. But – unlike in the early stages of the eastern legions – their volunteerism was in many cases an overwhelmingly opportunistic decision. It was simply more pleasant to be clothed, fed and paid like a German soldier than to starve behind barbed wire or die of spotted fever, especially as each man received 300 cigarettes when he signed up for the legion. By the way, the positive motivations were greater when the German military was on the advance than later, when there were only retreats and victory by the Soviets and the other Allied armies appeared unstoppable. The fact is, in war it is always more interesting to finish up on the side of the victor."

The Decoration for Bravery and Merit for Eastern Peoples

With the number of eastern volunteers rising rapidly and many of them already having distinguished themselves in action, the question arose how to honor their service. On 17 February 1942 the OKH released the following:

> *"For the time being, foreign volunteers from areas liberated from the Bolsheviks who are fighting under the command of the German military or in units of the German military may not receive war decorations, such as the Iron Cross, etc.*
>
> *On the other hand, assault badges and wound badges may be awarded to these volunteers as per the existing regulations."*

This meant, however, that acts of conspicuous bravery or special service could not be recognized. Not until five months later was this disadvantageous situation rectified and a new decoration created. On 22 July 1942, the *Reich Law Gazette* No.78 published Hitler's ordinance concerning the institution of the Decoration for Eastern Peoples:

> *"As a visible sign of recognition for bravery and merit, I establish the ...*
>
> *Decoration for Bravery and Merit for Eastern Peoples.*
>
> *As per my instructions, the head of the Wehrmacht High Command will issue the implementing regulations in consultation with the Minister of State and head of the Reich President's office.*
>
> *Führer Headquarters, 14 July 1942*
>
> *... Adolf Hitler ..."*

According to the award regulations, the decoration with swords was a decoration for bravery and without swords a merit decoration. Tsarist decoration stars probably served as inspiration in designing the decoration. There were two classes with different grades. While the 1st Class was a pin badge which could only be awarded in silver and gold, the 2nd Class decoration was awarded in bronze on a dark green ribbon, in silver on a green ribbon edged in white, and in gold on a pale green ribbon edged in red. As a further reference to Tsarist decorations, each class was awarded in sequence of grades, and each grade could be awarded up to three times.

In special cases, special monetary or other property awards could accompany the awarding of the 1st Class. Such applications had to be submitted to the OKH/PA.

The Decoration for Bravery and Merit for Eastern Peoples 1st and 2nd Classes in Silver were awarded for approximately the same number of acts as the Iron Crosses, First and Second Class and the War Merit Crosses, First and Second Class. The 2nd Class in bronze could be awarded in recognition of a minor action, while the 2nd Class in Gold had to be awarded for several actions that were not, however, sufficient for the awarding of the 1st Class in Silver. To earn the 1st Class in Gold, the foreign soldier had to have performed conspicuously several times.

The 2nd Class decorations were on a ribbon that could be attached to the uniform by means of a safety pin. They were only worn on special occasions, however. Otherwise a small field bar was worn. This was comparable, for example, to the Commemorative Medal for 13 March 1938. With a diameter of about four centimeters, the two classes were smaller than the 1st Class pin cross, which was about five centimeters in size. Two versions of the decoration were produced, normally in refined zinc: a sculpted version with a deepening the size of the medallion on the reverse, resulting in a raised obverse, and a flat one without the latter feature. While in some cases the manufacturer's code 100 is engraved on the ribbon ring or reverse side of the pin on the first version, the flat version lacks any kind of manufacturer's marking. It is interesting to note that the bravery and merit decoration was the only German decoration of its type without a swastika.

While the 2nd Class grades were presented to recipients in the award packaging, as a rule those awarded the 1st class were also given an award case.

The decoration could be awarded to:

Turkish units
Cossack units
Crimean Tatar units
Auxiliary Police (*Schutzmannschaft*) Battalions
Unarmed auxiliaries (*Hilfswilligen*, or *Hiwis*) in German units
Domestic security units in the operations zone.

Not eligible were:

Inhabitants who served only briefly as auxiliaries
Prisoners of war.

The decorations for bravery were awarded by the nearest *Wehrmacht* officer in command of at least a division or by the Senior SS and Police Commander, while the merit decorations were initially awarded by the Reich Minister for the Occupied Eastern Territories. This authority to award the decoration changed, at the latest when foreign units were moved to the south and west. After this, the closest officer in command of at least a division was also entitled to award the merit decorations. For auxiliaries serving in the *Kriegsmarine*, the decorations were awarded by the Commander-in-Chief of Naval Group Commands and Navy High Command.

The award requirements were modified on 28 May 1943. Whereas hitherto eastern volunteers were generally only awarded decorations for eastern peoples, those who had sworn an oath to Hitler and were fighting within the German military could now also be decorated with the Iron Cross and the War Merit Cross, in addition to branch of service badges and wound badges. To be awarded the Iron Cross, Second Class or First Class, the recipient had to first have received the bravery decoration second class or first class. To receive the various grades of the War Merit Cross, the candidate had to be in possession of the corresponding merit decoration in silver.

At the same time, German soldiers could now be awarded the bravery and merit decoration "*to visibly emphasize the decoration's value to members of the eastern peoples.*" In this case it was not a decoration in the conventional sense, instead it was a medal for German core personnel who served in eastern units. The award requirements were the exactly the reverse of those for the awarding of the Iron Cross and War Merit Cross to eastern volunteers. The German candidate had to be in possession of the Iron Cross, Second Class or First Class for the bravery decoration second or first class in silver, or the War Merit Cross, Second or First Class for the merit decoration second or first class.

SS-Standartenführer Lammerding, commander of SS Battle Group von Gottberg, announced these changes to the battalions under his command on 21 November 1943. In awarding German decorations, however, he based his decisions not on having sworn the oath to Hitler, but instead on the ethnic origins of the candidate. This was probably an error in interpretation:

> "... *Provided the remaining requirements are met, the bravery decorations for Eastern Peoples [can] then also be awarded to liaison (supervisory) officers and to the German auxiliary personnel in Schutzmannschaft battalions that are engaged in combat, and to all German members who have been given command tasks in such battalions.*

> *Condition for the award is possession of the Iron Cross, Second (First) Class 1939 or the bar to the Iron Cross, Second (First) Class or their awarding. In the latter case the decoration for bravery will also be awarded.*
>
> *Awarding of the "Decoration for Bravery and Merit for Eastern Peoples" to Lithuanians, Latvians or Estonians is out of the question. In matters of conspicuous bravery or war service, they are subject to the same conditions for the awarding of war decorations as Germans."*

The way the decorations were awarded is interesting. The statute states that: *"until the badges and certificates are delivered, the band is to be issued and worn, and temporary certificates are to be presented by the awarding offices."* In practice this meant that it was actually battalion and regiment commanders who had the authority to award decorations. This is born out by the following report by the SS and Police Commander White Russia on 6 July 1943:

> *"To Auxiliary Police Battalions 15, 54, 57, 102, 118 and SS-Bataillon-Dirlewanger:*
>
> *Subject: Prompt submission of recommendations for the awarding of the Decoration for Bravery and Merit for Eastern Peoples from Operation Cottbus as per the order of 5 June 1943.*
>
> *In the letter, make note of who has already received the decoration from those already on hand there, so that the document can be drawn up."*

Reference to this unusual manner of awarding the decoration can also be found in the history of the VX Cossack Cavalry Corps:

> *"For the alertness and bravery displayed in the fighting on Christmas Eve 1943, the regimental commander was able to award decorations from his personal stock that same night. Requests for approval of these will subsequently have to be submitted to the division."*

Commanders who were familiar with the mentality of the foreign volunteers also handed out small gifts when decorations were presented. While foreign volunteers were very proud to be honored with the decoration, possession of a watch or the enjoyment of a bottle of liquor was a special incentive for them and their comrades. The following appears in the war diary of the III Battalion, *Waffen-Grenadier-Regiment der SS 76 (russ.Nr.5)* on 3 October 1944:

> *"Practice attack in battalion formation. Afterwards the division commander arrived to decorate two grenadiers with the Decoration for Bravery and Merit for Eastern Peoples in Bronze. At the same time, these men were each given a watch and a bottle of schnapps as a reward for the clever capture of two agents..."*

The former adjutant of *Kosaken-Artillerie-Regiment 55*, *Oberleutnant* Karl Gottfried Vierkorn, remembered:

> *"When the Cossack division was formed, as a new Leutnant I was made a platoon leader in an artillery battery, then a short time later in the Balkans I was placed in command of a battery, and in the spring of 1944 I became adjutant (first battalion, then regiment). As its name suggests, the Decoration for Bravery and Merit for Eastern Peoples was actually created just for them. However, the silver grade was also awarded to officers as well as to several NCOs who fought with the foreigners – in my case Cossacks."*

With a total number of more than three-quarters of a million eastern volunteers during the course of the war and a corresponding number of German core personnel, one can conclude that the Decoration for Bravery and Merit for Eastern Peoples was awarded about 100,000 times. The 2nd Class in Bronze and Silver was relatively common. While the version in Gold was much less common, the 1st Class in Silver and Gold was extremely rare. One known wearer of the 1st Class was *Brigadegeneral* Bronislav Kaminski, the commander of RONA, the Russian People's Liberation Army.

Bibliography

Reichsgesetzblatt Nr.78 vom 22.July 1942
Allgemeine Heeresmitteilungen 1942 Nr.667
Marine-Berdordnungsblatt 1943 Nr.98
Anlagen zum III./Waffen-Grenadier-Regiments der SS 76 (russ.Nr.5)

Gritzner, *Maximilian, Handbuch der Ritter- und Verdienstorden*, Leipzig, 1981.

Kalben, Heinrich-Detloff, Wagner, Constantin, *Die Geschichte des XV.Kos.Kav.Korps.*

Michaelis, Rolf, *Die Verwundetenabzeichen 1918-1936-1939*, Erlangen, 1995.

Michaelis, Rolf, *Die Sturmabzeichen des Heeres*, Erlangen, 1996.

Michaelis, Rolf, *Die Nahkampfspange des Heeres*, Erlangen, 1996.

Michaelis, Rolf, *Das Bandenkampfabzeichen*, Erlangen, 1997.

Schlicht, Adolf, Angolia, John, *Die Deutsche Wehrmacht*, Stuttgart, 1992.

Ten thousand prisoners of war, former members of the Red Army, volunteered to serve with the Germans in 1941-42. In addition to Ukrainians, Balts and Caucasians, there were also Asians. For most, volunteering was a way to escape starvation in the POW camps.

Service club for members of the Volga Tatar Legion.

Officers of the Turkestan Legion.

Goebbels and members of the XV Cossack Cavalry Corps.

The Order of St. Alexander Nevsky. Instituted on 21 May 1725 by Russian Empress Catherine I, it bears a striking similarity to the Decoration for Bravery and Merit for Eastern Peoples.

Decoration for Bravery Second Class in Bronze (green ribbon), obverse.

Reverse with medallion depression.

Decoration for Bravery Second Class in Silver (green ribbon with white stripes).

Reverse with no medallion depression.

Merit Decoration Second Class in Gold (green ribbon with red stripes).

Reverse with medallion depression.

Merit Decoration First Class in Silver.

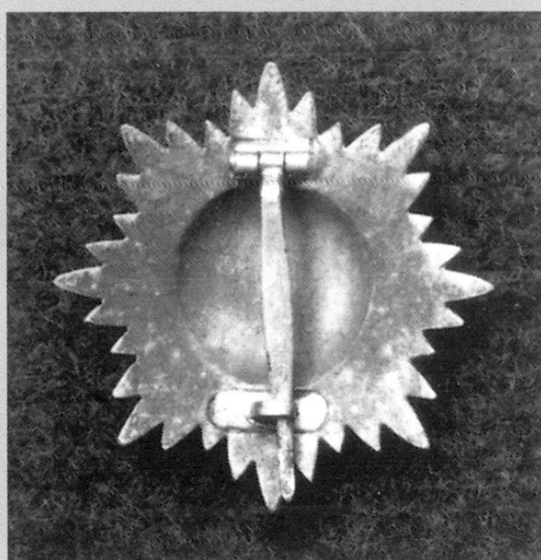

Decoration for Bravery First Class in Gold

Reverse of the First Class decoration with medallion depression.

Raised version (deepening of medallion)

Flat version (no deepening of medallion)

Decoration for Bravery
in Presentation Case

Merit Decoration
in Presentation Case

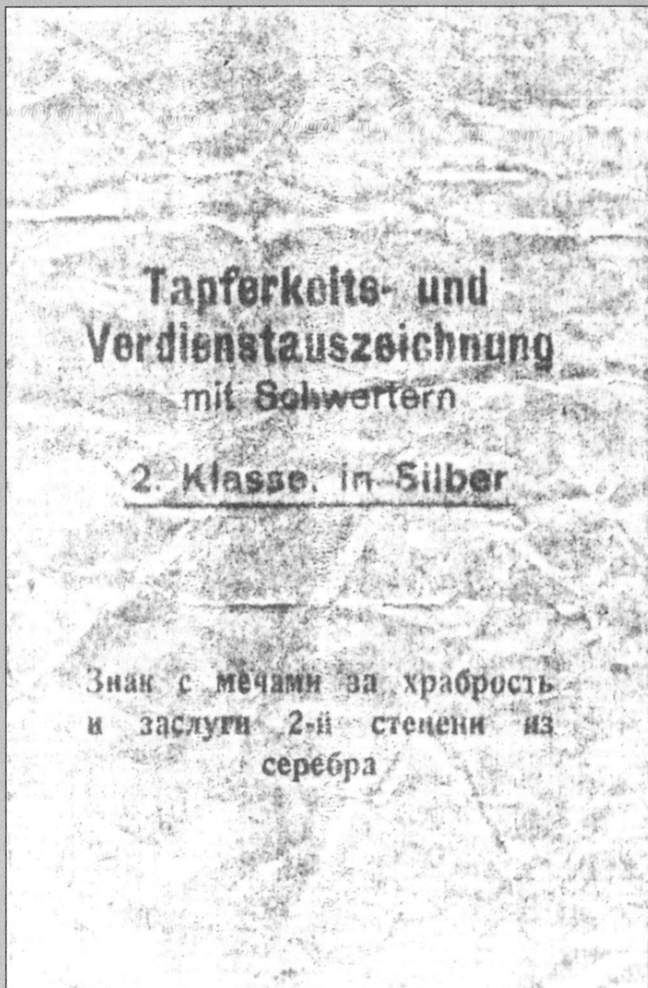

Award packet with German-Russian script.

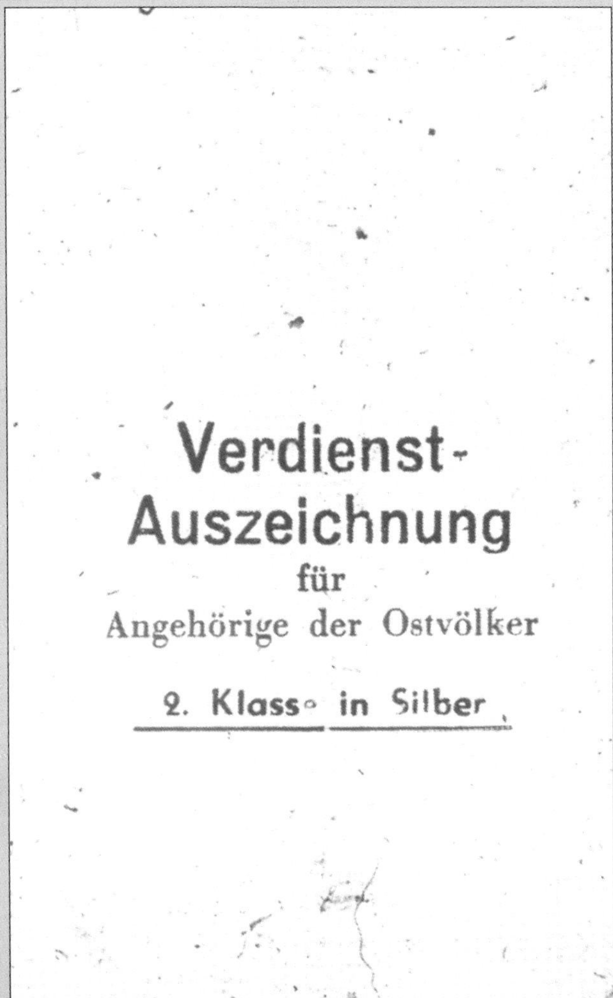

Award packet for the Merit Decoration for Eastern Peoples Second Class in Silver.

Award packet for the Merit Decoration for Eastern Peoples Second Class in Gold.

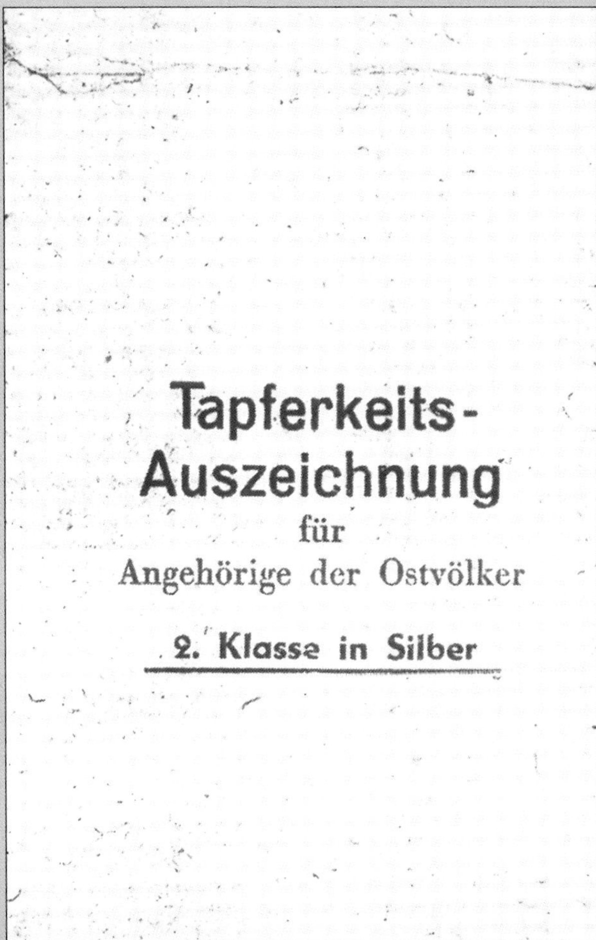

Tapferkeits-
Auszeichnung
für
Angehörige der Ostvölker

2. Klasse in Silber

Award packet for the Decoration for Bravery for Eastern Peoples Second Class in Silver.

Tapferkeits-
Auszeichnung
für
Angehörige der Ostvölker
1. Klasse in Silber

Award packet for the Decoration for Bravery for Eastern Peoples First Class in Silver.

Hans Wohlmuth was awarded the Decoration for Bravery for Eastern Peoples Second Class in Silver while serving with the Siberian Cossacks as a member of the German support personnel.

An Estonian volunteer of an eastern battalion wearing the ribbons for the Eastern Medal and the Decoration for Bravery and Merit for Eastern Peoples 2nd Class in Bronze.

Interestingly this Estonian officer of an eastern battalion is wearing both Iron Crosses, Second and First Class, in addition to the Decoration for Bravery and Merit for Eastern Peoples 2nd Class in Bronze.

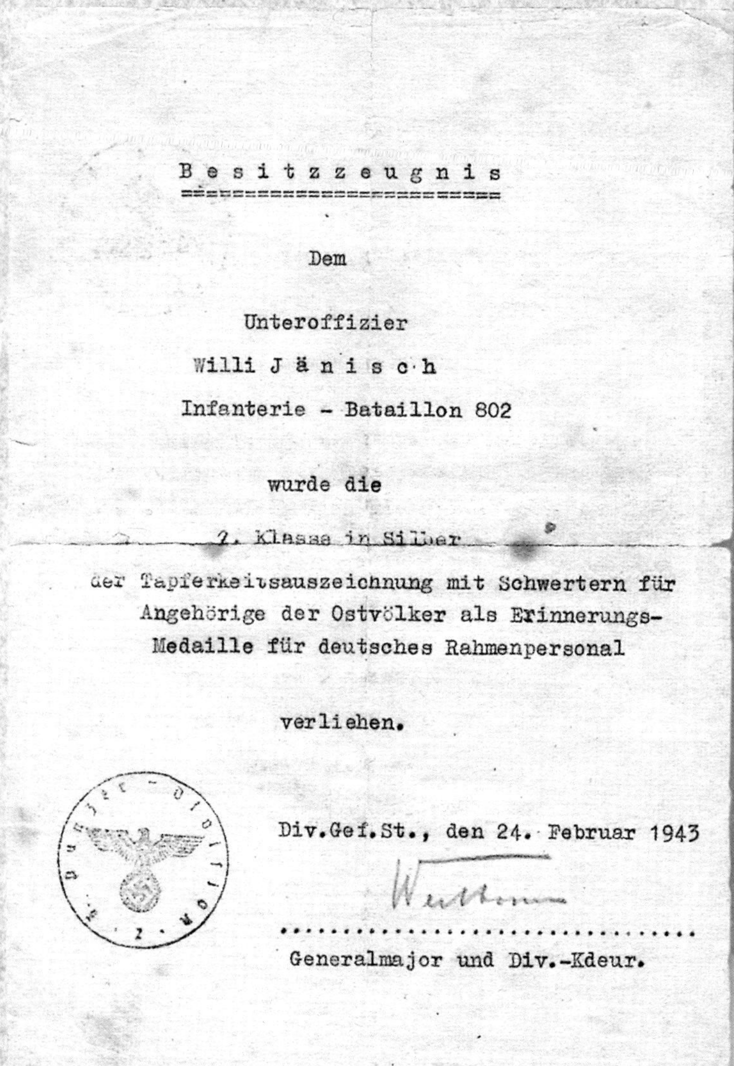

B e s i t z z e u g n i s

Dem

Unteroffizier

Willi J ä n i s c h

Infanterie - Bataillon 802

wurde die

2. Klasse in Silber

der Tapferkeitsauszeichnung mit Schwertern für Angehörige der Ostvölker als Erinnerungs-Medaille für deutsches Rahmenpersonal

verliehen.

Div.Gef.St., den 24. Februar 1943

Generalmajor und Div.-Kdeur.

This award document specifically states that the decoration was awarded as a commemorative medal for German support personnel.

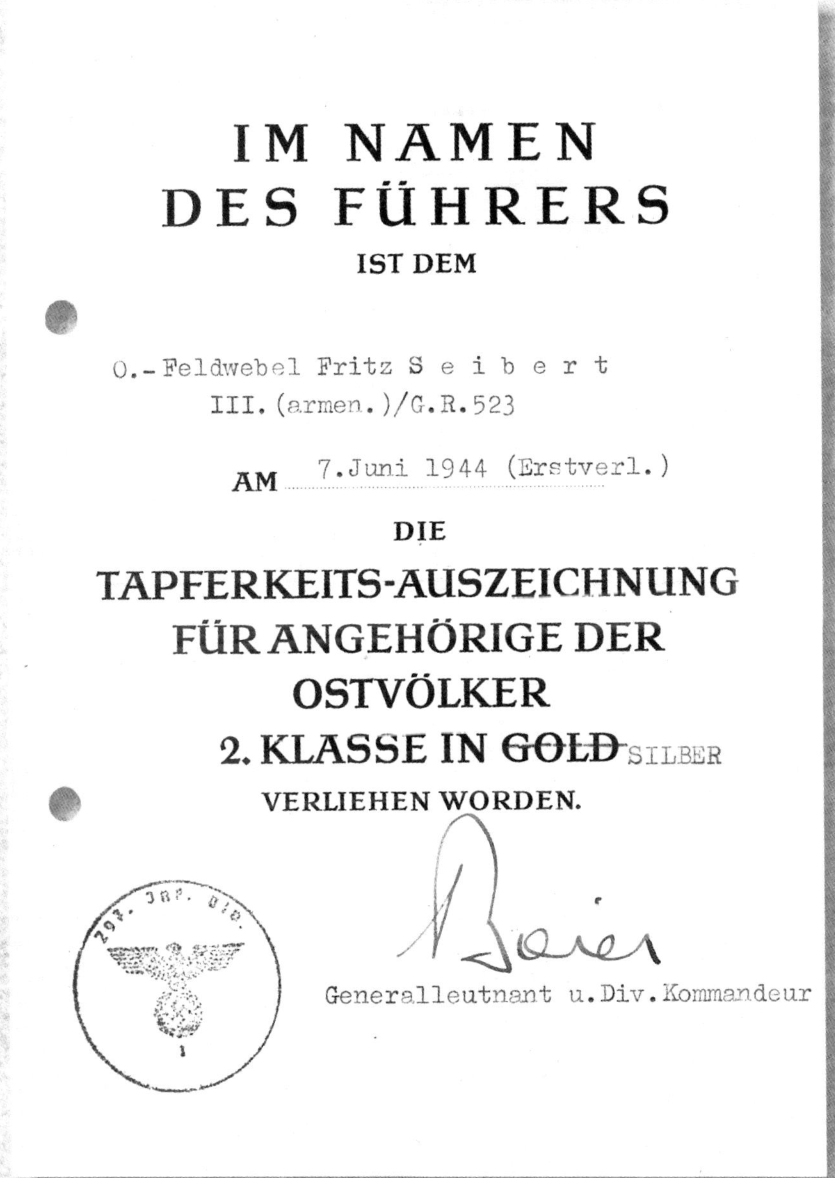

IM NAMEN
DES FÜHRERS
IST DEM

O.-Feldwebel Fritz S e i b e r t
III. (armen.)/G.R.523

AM 7.Juni 1944 (Erstverl.)

DIE

TAPFERKEITS-AUSZEICHNUNG
FÜR ANGEHÖRIGE DER
OSTVÖLKER
2. KLASSE IN ~~GOLD~~ SILBER

VERLIEHEN WORDEN.

Baier

Generalleutnant u.Div.Kommandeur

Interestingly, shown here is the addition of the words "first awarding" – the headquarters staff was probably unaware that the decoration was only supposed to be awarded once to German core personnel.

Russian volunteers about to be decorated.

Orden und Ehrenzeichen

Datum	Art der Auszeichnung	Urkunde erhalten	Bestätigung (Komp.- usw. Führer)
20.4.44.	K.v.K. 2.Kl. m. Schwertern	20.4.44	[illegible]
1.6.44	Bandenkampf-abz. i. Bronze		[illegible]
15.8.44	[illegible] f. Angeh. v. [illegible]		[illegible]

From a pay book: in addition to the War Merit Cross 2nd Class with Swords and the Anti-Partisan War Badge in Bronze, this German SS member was awarded the Merit Decoration for Eastern Peoples 2nd Class in Silver.

Probably one of the best known wearers of the Decoration for Bravery for Eastern Peoples, the leader of the Russian People's Liberation Army, (RONA) Brigadeführer Bronislav Kaminski.

A Caucasian volunteer wearing the ribbon of the Decoration for Bravery and Merit for Eastern Peoples 2nd Class in Bronze.

Approximately 6,000 Lithuanian volunteers served in the German military and were eligible to receive the Decoration for Bravery and Merit for Eastern Peoples. This volunteer is wearing the sleeve badge with the Lithuanian title for his nation: "Lietuva."

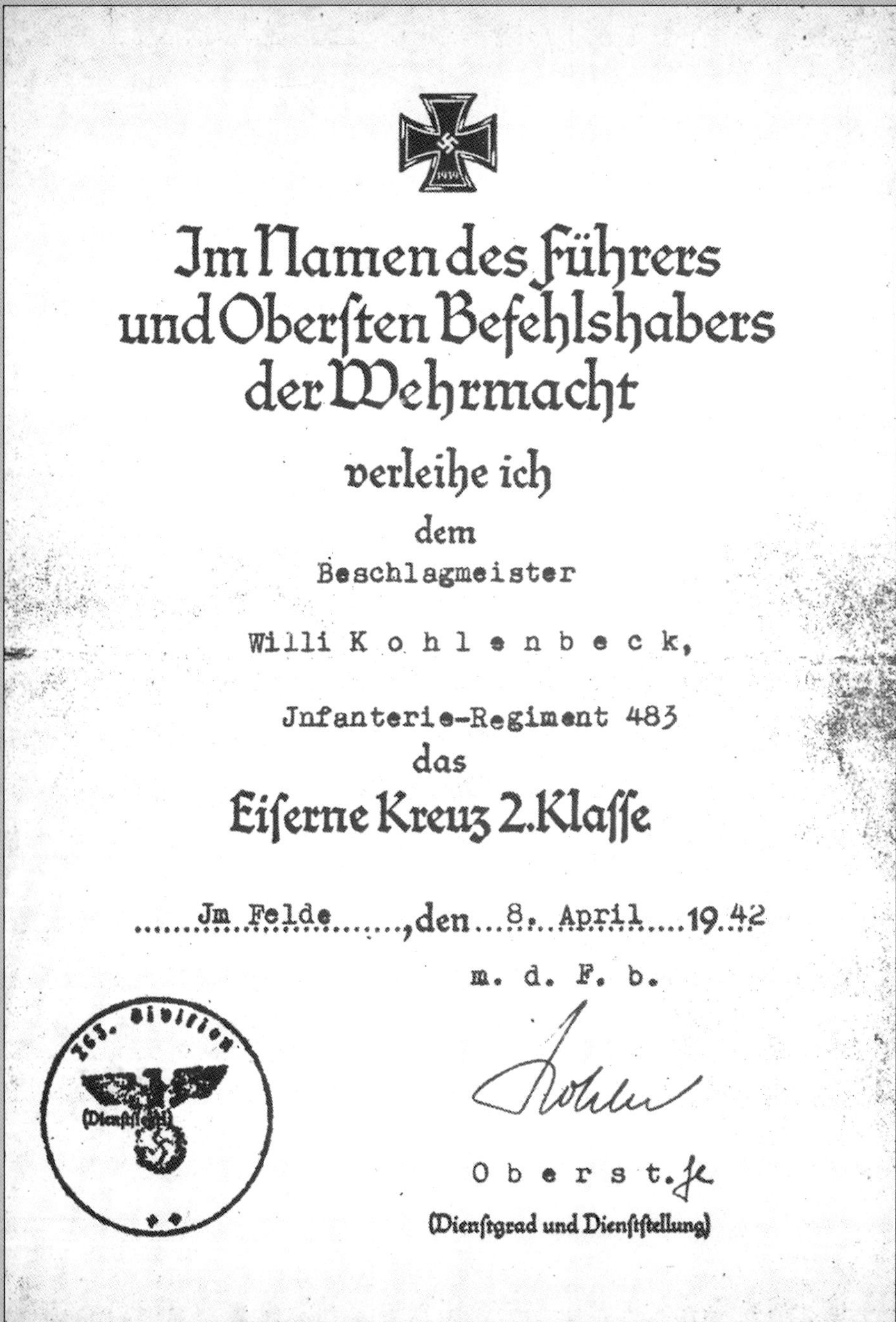

Im Namen des Führers und Obersten Befehlshabers der Wehrmacht

verleihe ich

dem

Beschlagmeister

Willi Kohlenbeck,

Jnfanterie-Regiment 483

das

Eiserne Kreuz 2. Klasse

Jm Felde, den 8. April 1942

m. d. F. b.

Kohler

Oberst.

(Dienstgrad und Dienststellung)

IM NAMEN
DES FÜHRERS
IST DEM

Oberbeschlagmeister
Wilhelm K o h l e n b e c k

AM 23.August 1943

DIE

TAPFERKEITS-AUSZEICHNUNG
FÜR ANGEHÖRIGE DER
OSTVÖLKER
2. KLASSE IN SILBER
VERLIEHEN WORDEN.

Generaloberst

IM NAMEN DES FÜHRERS
VERLEIHE ICH
DEM

Oberbeschlagmeister
Wilhelm K o h l e n b e c k
(Kos.) Gren. Rgt. 360

DAS
EISERNE KREUZ
1. KLASSE

K.Gef.Std., 15. Sept. 1944

Der Kommandierende General

Generalleutnant
(DIENSTGRAD UND DIENSTSTELLUNG)

IM NAMEN
DES FÜHRERS
IST DEM

Oberbeschlagmeister Wilhelm Kohlenbeck

Stab (Kos.) Gren. Rgt. 360

AM 12. Nov. 1944
DIE

TAPFERKEITS-AUSZEICHNUNG
FÜR ANGEHÖRIGE DER
OSTVÖLKER
1. KLASSE IN SILBER
VERLIEHEN WORDEN.

K.Gef.St., den 12. 11. 1944

General der Flieger und
Kommandierender General

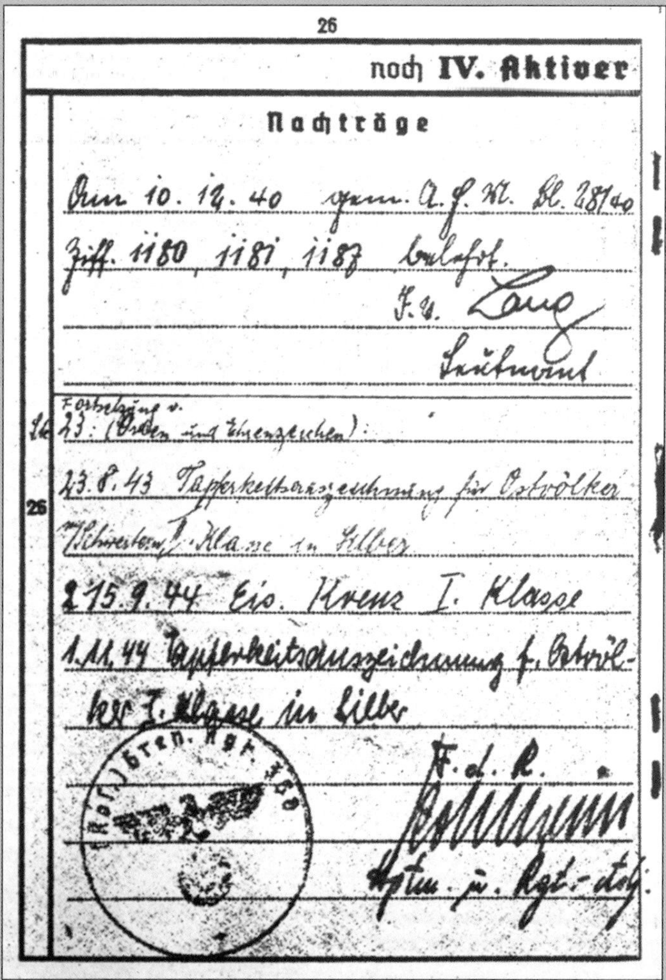

26

noch IV. Aktiver

Nachträge

Am 10. 12. 40 gem. A.f.M. Bl. 28/40

Ziff. 1180, 1181, 1187 berichtigt.

F.d. Lang

Leutnant

26 Fortsetzung v. 23: (Orden und Ehrenzeichen):

23.8.43 Tapferkeitsauszeichnung für Ostvölker

(Schwerter) I. Klasse in Silber

15.9.44 Eis. Kreuz I. Klasse

1.11.44 Tapferkeitsauszeichnung f. Ostvölker I. Klasse in Silber

F.d.R.

Hptm. u. Rgt.-Adj.

A page from a service book showing the awarding of the Decoration for Bravery and Merit for Eastern Peoples.

A former lieutenant in the Estonian Army, in September 1942 Viktor Sihver volunteered to serve in the German military. In the spring of 1944 he was transferred to the 20. Waffen-Grenadier-Division der SS (estnische Nr.1).

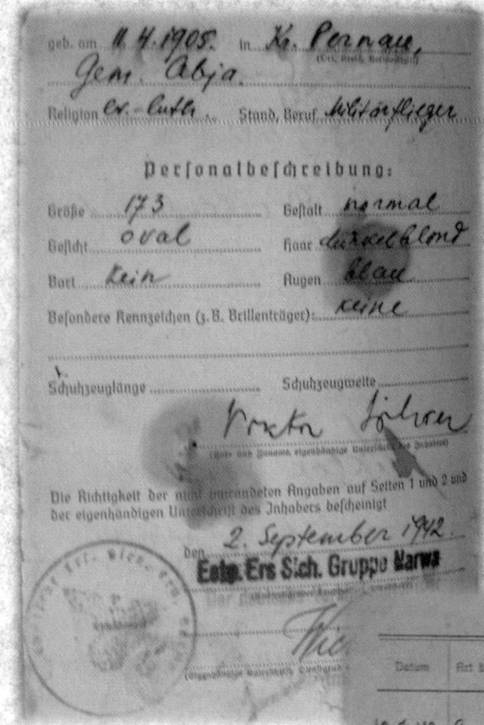

geb. am 11.4.1905 in Kr. Pernau, Gem. Abja

Religion ev.-luth. Stand, Beruf Militärflieger

Personalbeschreibung:

Größe 173 Gestalt normal

Gesicht oval Haar dunkelblond

Bart kein Augen blau

Besondere Kennzeichen (z.B. Brillenträger): keine

Schuhzeuglänge .... Schuhzeugweite ....

(Vor- und Zuname, eigenhändige Unterschrift des Inhabers)

Die Richtigkeit der nicht umrandeten Angaben auf Seiten 1 und 2 und der eigenhändigen Unterschrift des Inhabers bescheinigt

den 2. September 1942.

Estn. Ers. Sich. Gruppe Narwa

(Eigenhändige Unterschrift)

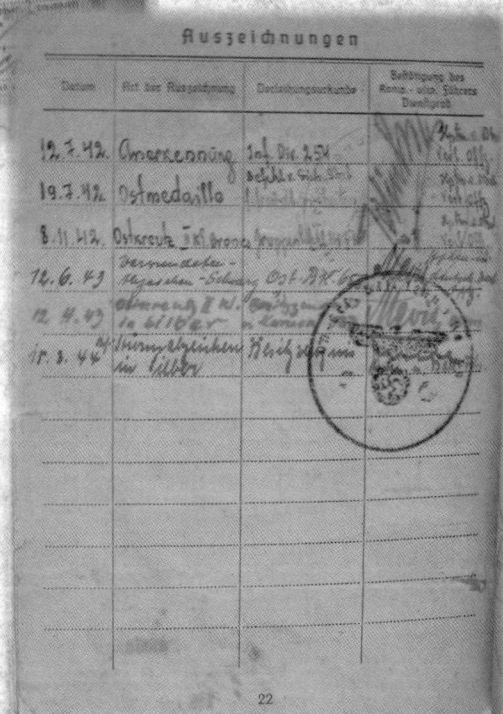

Auszeichnungen

Datum	Art der Auszeichnung	Verleihungsurkunde	Bestätigung des Komp.- usw. Führers Dienstgrad
12.7.42	Anerkennung	Inf. Div. 254	
19.7.42	Ostmedaille		
8.11.42	Ostkreuz II Kl. Bronze		
12.6.43	Verwundeten-Abzeichen-Schwarz		
12.4.43	Ostkreuz II Kl. in Silber		
15.3.44	Sturmabzeichen in Silber		

22

Sihver received a commendation from the commander of the 254th Infantry Division, the Eastern Medal, the Wound Badge in Black and, in addition to the Infantry Assault Badge, two Decorations for Bravery for Eastern Peoples, which here are called "East Crosses."

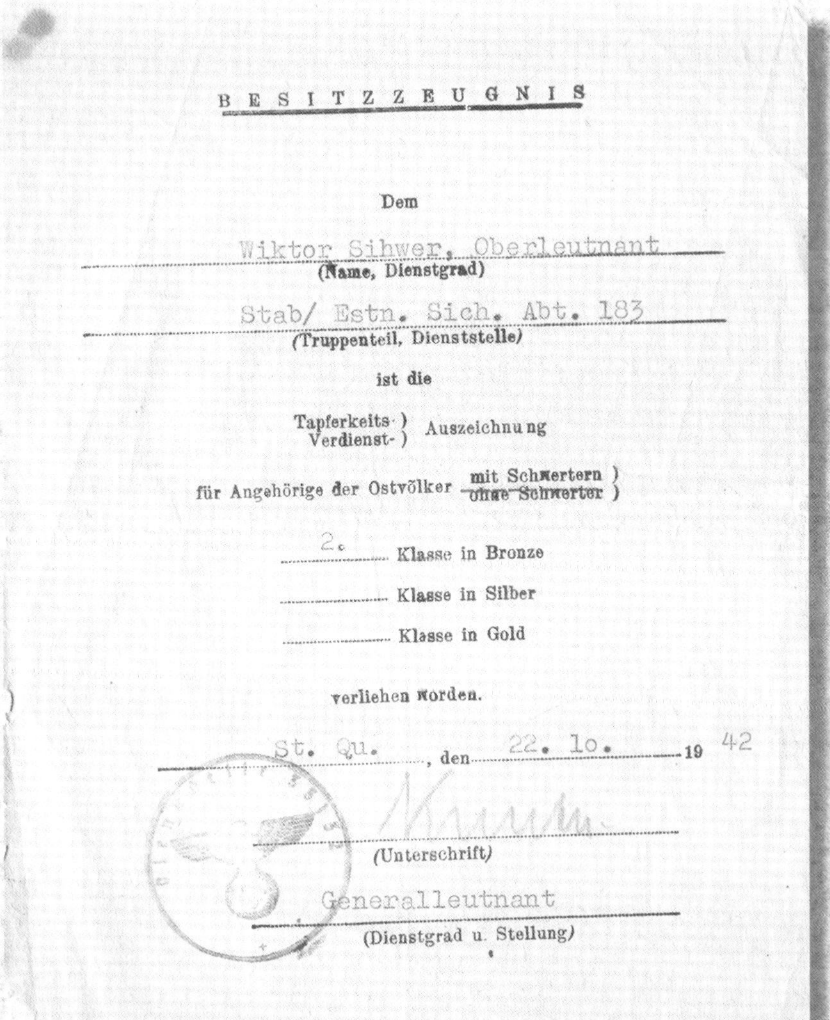

B E S I T Z Z E U G N I S

Dem

Wiktor Sihwer, Oberleutnant
(Name, Dienstgrad)

Stab/ Estn. Sich. Abt. 183
(Truppenteil, Dienststelle)

ist die

Tapferkeits-)
Verdienst-) Auszeichnung

für Angehörige der Ostvölker mit Schwertern)
~~ohne Schwerter~~)

2. Klasse in Bronze

.... Klasse in Silber

.... Klasse in Gold

verliehen worden.

St. Qu., den 22. 10. 1942

(Unterschrift)

Generalleutnant
(Dienstgrad u. Stellung)

Interesting version of an award certificate for the various Decorations for Bravery and Merit for Eastern Peoples.

The owner of this pay book received:

20/04/1942 the Wound Badge in Black
24/07/1942 the East Medal
08/11/1942 the Decoration for Bravery and Merit for Eastern Peoples 2nd Class in Bronze
11/02/1943 the Decoration for Bravery and Merit for Eastern Peoples 2nd Class in Silver
08/04/1943 the Iron Cross, Second Class
12/05/1943 the Infantry Assault Badge
16/02/1944 the Iron Cross, First Class
20/04/1944 the Wound Badge in Silver